State Governments

Lisa Perlman Greathouse

Consultant

Brian Allman
Principal
Upshur County Schools, West Virginia

Publishing Credits

Rachelle Cracchiolo, M.S.Ed., *Publisher*
Emily R. Smith, M.A.Ed., *SVP of Content Development*
Véronique Bos, *VP of Creative*
Dona Herweck Rice, *Senior Content Manager*
Dani Neiley, *Editor*
Fabiola Sepulveda, *Series Graphic Designer*

Image Credits: p5 Library of Congress [LC-H8- P03-001-A]; p7 Library of Congress [14021670]; p8 Shutterstock/JessicaGirvan; p10 Shutterstock/Eli Wilson; p13–14 Shutterstock/Jonathan Weiss; p17 (top) Shutterstock/Blueee77; p19 Shutterstock/Alex Millauer; p20 Shutterstock/Rob Crandall; p21 Library of Congress [LC-DIG-ggbain-12924]; p30–31 Shutterstock/Mroald; p32 Library of Congress [LC-DIG-hec-47235]; all other images from iStock and/or Shutterstock

Library of Congress Cataloging-in-Publication Data

Names: Greathouse, Lisa E., author.
Title: State governments / Lisa Perlman Greathouse.
Description: Huntington Beach, CA : Teacher Created Materials, 2023. | Includes index. | Audience: Grades 4-6 | Summary: "When it comes to having power in government, you might think of the president. But who decides how old you need to be to drive or what educators teach in school? Who takes care of making sure the air and water are clean? In most cases, it is the state government and its leaders who make decisions that directly affect citizens' lives"-- Provided by publisher.
Identifiers: LCCN 2022021237 (print) | LCCN 2022021238 (ebook) | ISBN 9781087691107 (paperback) | ISBN 9781087691268 (ebook)
Subjects: LCSH: State governments--United States--Juvenile literature.
Classification: LCC JK2408 .G738 2023 (print) | LCC JK2408 (ebook) | DDC 320.473--dc23/eng/20220601
LC record available at https://lccn.loc.gov/2022021237
LC ebook record available at https://lccn.loc.gov/2022021238

Shown on the cover is the New Hampshire State House.

TCM Teacher Created Materials
5482 Argosy Avenue
Huntington Beach, CA 92649
www.tcmpub.com

ISBN 978-1-0876-9110-7

Table of Contents

view of the Colorado State Capitol from inside a judicial building

“In Between” Government

What comes to mind when you hear the word *government*? You might think of the president or Congress. They are part of the U.S. federal government. You might think of a city council or the mayor. They are part of the local government. You might even have a student government at school.

In between local and federal governments is the state government. There is a state government for each state. Each has its own **constitution**, which includes state laws not covered by the federal government. States can make their own laws if they do not go against the U.S. Constitution.

No matter what size the state is, its state government is set up the same way. Like the federal government, each has three branches: executive, legislative, and judicial. (More on those later.)

All levels of government affect the lives of people. But in many ways, state governments have the biggest influence on people’s everyday lives. Let’s find out why.

inside the Texas State Capitol

A Great Compromise

States with the biggest populations send more leaders to the U.S. House of Representatives. California has the highest population, with almost 40 million people, and elects 53 U.S. representatives. Wyoming has about 580,000 residents and elects only one representative. But both states elect two U.S. senators. This system was part of the Great **Compromise** made during the 1787 Constitutional Convention.

Person at the Top

Just as schools need principals and teams need coaches, every U.S. state needs a leader. Governors are these leaders. They are the state's chief executives. That means they are like presidents of their states.

Every state has its own constitution, so the rules and powers of the governor differ from state to state. Governors make decisions that affect the lives of people in their states, no matter where they live. Governors decide how to spend the state's money. They can promote issues that are important to them, such as building schools and roads. They are also in charge of the state's military. When there is a flood or another natural disaster, the governor must take charge. They can declare an emergency to get funds to help people rebuild their lives.

Engineers' Pay per 100 Miles.

	1897	1913	Increase Per Cent.	Avg. Pay Per Month
Passenger............	$3 00	$4 40	46.7	$230 16
Through Freight......	4 00	5 25	31.3	
Mallet Eng...........		6 50	62.5	180 00
Local Freight........	4 00	5 50	37.5	

1914 Virginia bill

Firemen's Pay per 100 Miles.

	1897	1913	Increase Per Cent.	Avg. Pay Per Month
Passenger............	$1 50	$2 50	66.7	$128 65
Through Freight......	1 75	3 10	77.1	
Mallet Eng...........		4 00	128.6	118 54
Local Freight........	1 75	3 25	85.7	

You will observe that this statement shows the *average* pay per month that employees in train service can make by working full time.

The result of the increased wages and expenses of train service has been that the cost per train mile of handling freight has more than doubled during this period:

In 1897 the cost per freight train mile....... $1 02
In 1913 the cost per freight train mile....... 2 10

During this period the revenue received from hauling passengers and freight have decreased as follows:

	1897	1913	Decrease Per Cent.
Revenue per passenger per mile—cents..............	3.179	2.617	17.678
Revenue per ton freight per mile—cents..............	.445	.429	3.59

From these comparative figures it is apparent that in the face of increased wages and costs of operation, the only way to increase revenue, not proportionately, but at all

State lawmakers work to pass bills. Those bills become law only if the governor signs them. A governor can also **veto** a bill. In some states, lawmakers have the power to overturn a veto through a two-thirds vote.

Not Old Enough to Vote, but Old Enough to Run

In Vermont, there is no age restriction for candidates for governor. In 2018, 14-year-old Ethan Sonneborn ran for governor of Vermont. He lost the Democratic **primary**, but he's on his way to a career in politics!

18+ ONLY

How Governors Govern

The governor's job is to do what's best for the *whole* state—and that can be tricky. Sometimes, things can get in the way of a governor doing their job. For instance, in 2020, the world was first facing the COVID-19 **pandemic**. Each governor had to make tough decisions for their state. They decided whether it was safe for schools to stay open. They decided whether wearing masks was optional or required. No matter what their governor decided, some people were not happy.

The rules for who can become governor and how many years they can serve differ from state to state. Most states require governors to be at least 25 or 30 years old. But in Ohio and a few other states, you can be elected at just 18 years old—or even younger!

Most states elect a governor every four years. If they run for and win a second term, they can serve a total of eight years. Some states even allow a governor to serve a third term if they wait at least four years in between. Many state lawmakers go on to become governor. And some governors have gone on to become president.

The Long and Short of It

Terry Branstad served 22 years as governor of Iowa, making him the longest-serving governor of all time. The shortest-serving governor was Hiram Bingham III of Connecticut. He served for just one day in 1925 before filling a **vacancy** in the U.S. Senate.

Next in Line

All U.S. presidents have a vice president. Similarly, most governors have a lieutenant governor. The lieutenant governor takes over if the governor dies or resigns. But there's more to the job than that.

Some lieutenant governors **preside** over the state senate. That can actually give them more influence than the governor has to pass bills.

Some governors and lieutenant governors are running mates. But they can run on their own, too. They might even be from rival **political** parties.

Virginia governor Glenn Youngkin talks to parents and students about school safety.

Delaware governor's office

There are many other leaders in a state's executive branch:

- The attorney general speaks for the state in court.
- The secretary of state takes care of public records and serves as chief of elections.
- The treasurer invests and pays out state funds.
- An auditor makes sure that officials spend public money legally.

Other leaders include the superintendent of education, who makes decisions about schools. Some leaders work to keep the state's air and water clean. Others work on public-health issues. The way in which leaders run these departments can affect the quality of life for people of that state. Thousands of people work in state government.

A Lieutenant Governor Who Really Loved His Job

In Tennessee, the state senate chooses the lieutenant governor. John S. Wilder attained that post in 1971 and served until 2007. That's 36 years! He passed away in 2010 at age 88. He was one of the longest-serving legislative leaders in the world.

What Do State Legislators Do?

Have you ever wondered who decides what age someone needs to be to get a driver's license or how long a school day should be?

States decide these rules. State **legislators** create them. In all 50 states, citizens elect people to represent the districts they live in. Then, these representatives vote on issues that affect the whole state. Almost all states have two **chambers**, just like Congress. The state Senate is the smaller, upper chamber. Its members serve longer terms (usually four years). The House of Representatives is the bigger, lower chamber. Other terms for this group might be the Assembly or House of Delegates. Its members often serve for two years.

Most members usually belong to one of two major political parties. Some are Democrats, and others are Republicans. A few others belong to smaller third parties. State legislators can introduce bills they would like to see become laws. They also manage the state budget. Members are responsible for making sure residents of their districts have a voice in matters. Some state legislatures work all year, while others are part-time. They meet in their state capitol buildings.

Indiana state representatives stand for a moment of silence.

Some Legislature Facts

All states have a two-house legislature—called **bicameral** government—except for Nebraska. This state has a single, or **unicameral**, chamber. Salaries for state legislators range from over $100,000 per year (California and New York) to just $100 per year (New Hampshire).

Making the Case for State Courts

Every state has a constitution and a legislature that makes laws. But what happens when there is an accusation of someone breaking those laws? That's when the third branch of state government—the judicial system—steps in.

Special Courts

Some states have courts that handle specific legal matters. Family courts deal with adoptions, divorces, and other family matters. Other courts oversee issues surrounding wills after someone dies or **bankruptcy** when people or organizations do not have money to pay debts.

The Judiciary Act of 1789 was signed into law. This established the federal courts as separate from state courts. The young nation wanted to make sure that individual rights were protected. The courts allow anyone who suspects a violation of their liberties to appear in court and have a fair trial. When a legislator files a criminal or a **civil** case, it starts in the state's trial court. There can be hundreds of these courts in any state. They may handle thousands of cases each year. In fact, more than 90 percent of all court proceedings take place at the state level. A judge or a jury hears the case. Rulings are to be based on law—not on opinion or politics.

If someone thinks that a court's **verdict** is unfair, they can appeal. Then, the case may go to a higher court, the state court of appeals. If it's appealed again, it may move to the federal level. Some cases are appealed all the way up to the U.S. Supreme Court. That's the highest court in the country.

In some states, judges are elected or appointed by the governor. Some appointments are for life!

Serving on a Jury

A jury is a group of people who decide the verdict of a court case. Most juries have 12 members. The court selects them from a list of registered voters or licensed drivers in the area where the trial takes place.

Some people may think that notice to serve on a jury is a **nuisance**. They may have to take time off from work or school. But jury duty is an important responsibility. The Sixth Amendment to the U.S. Constitution guarantees the right to a trial by jury. A jury's decision affects the lives of people in court.

members of a jury

Grand Juries

A grand jury is a special type of jury. This jury does not decide a final verdict. Instead, it investigates reported crimes and has the power to call people to testify. Then, its members decide whether criminal charges against someone should be filed.

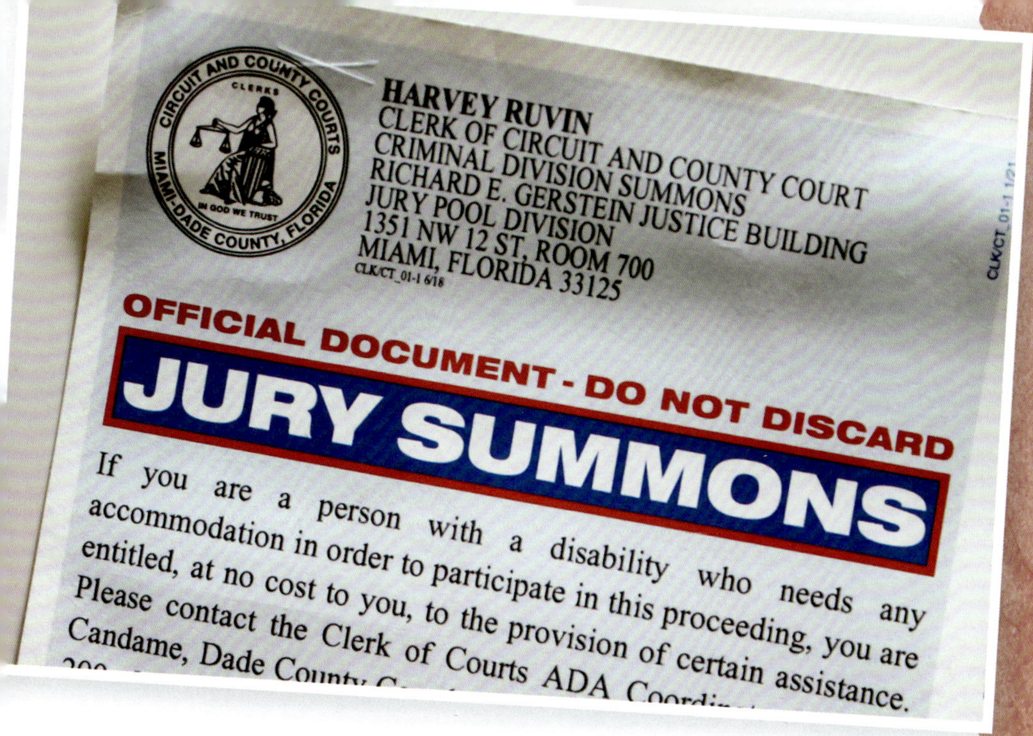

HARVEY RUVIN
CLERK OF CIRCUIT AND COUNTY COURT
CRIMINAL DIVISION SUMMONS
RICHARD E. GERSTEIN JUSTICE BUILDING
JURY POOL DIVISION
1351 NW 12 ST, ROOM 700
MIAMI, FLORIDA 33125

OFFICIAL DOCUMENT - DO NOT DISCARD
JURY SUMMONS

If you are a person with a disability who needs any accommodation in order to participate in this proceeding, you are entitled, at no cost to you, to the provision of certain assistance. Please contact the Clerk of Courts ADA Coordi... Candame, Dade County C...

Jurors must listen to hours, days—and sometimes weeks—of court proceedings. They must listen carefully to witnesses and experts. They may have to look at photos of crime scenes or review documents. They must avoid any news coverage of the case and may not discuss it with anyone else. In most cases, all jurors must agree on the verdict. If they cannot, the judge will declare a "hung jury." That puts an end to that trial, though the case may be retried with a new jury.

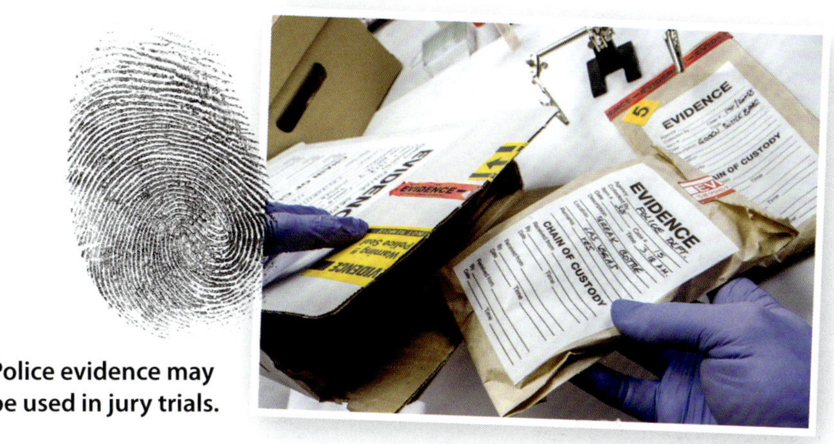

Police evidence may be used in jury trials.

Many Parts of State Governments

Where do people go to get a driver's license? Whom can you call if you want to get a pothole on the highway fixed? Where can you find out where to vote?

In most cases, the answer rests with the state government. There can be dozens of agencies within the state government. Some are big, like the Department of Education. Big agencies can have hundreds of employees.

The Many Names of Local Government

There are different names for local or **municipal** governments. In some places, they serve people who live in counties, boroughs, or villages. They may represent big cities with millions of people or towns with just a few hundred people.

There are times when responsibilities of the state overlap those of local governments. For instance, the local school board decides where to build schools. It hires teachers. But the state decides what subjects instructors will teach in public schools across the state. It also decides which tests all students need to take.

Government buildings are used to provide services for residents.

The Department of Motor Vehicles (DMV) is a state agency many people know well. They have to work with the DMV to get their first driver's licenses. Then, there is the Department of Transportation. State employees build and maintain highways in the state. They decide speed limits. The federal government oversees interstate highways. And local governments take care of the local roads. There are lots of overlaps like that, where duties are divided among the different levels of government.

Ensuring Fair Elections

Making sure each state has fair and honest elections is a crucial part of democracy. Citizens over 18 years old must be able to cast a ballot. Then, the vote count must be honest. Both those things are necessary if people are to trust elections of their leaders.

Local, state, and federal governments each have a role in elections. All states do things a little differently, but each has a chief election official. In some states, voters elect a secretary of state for that job. In others, the state legislature chooses the person. Many states have a commission to run elections.

Running elections is not easy! The state must keep a list of registered voters. Officials must design ballots. Candidates must receive certification. Other officials must test the voting machines and send them to poll sites. State officials need to make sure that everyone follows laws at polling places. For instance, most states do not allow voters to bring anything promoting a specific candidate to polling sites.

Virginia voters check in at their polling place.

Most importantly, state officials must count the votes. Then, they certify the winners. When elections are very close, a candidate may request a **recount**. Then, the state may need to count votes a second time—or even a third!

Women protest for the right to vote.

Fighting for the Right to Vote

When the United States was formed, only white men who owned property could vote. The 15th and 19th Amendments to the Constitution granted Black men the right to vote in 1870 and women the right to vote in 1920. Today, people who are citizens and are over 18 years old can vote.

The Electoral College

One of the toughest decisions for the Founders was how to elect a U.S. president. Some of them wanted Congress to pick the president. Others said it should be a vote of the people—whoever got the most votes would win. They wound up with a compromise. It is called the Electoral College.

Every four years, states choose a group of **electors**. Every state gets the same number of electors as it has representatives in Congress. So, California gets 55, while Vermont gets 3. In most states, all electors vote for whomever wins the most votes. There are 538 electors in all; the candidate who gets at least 270 votes is the winner.

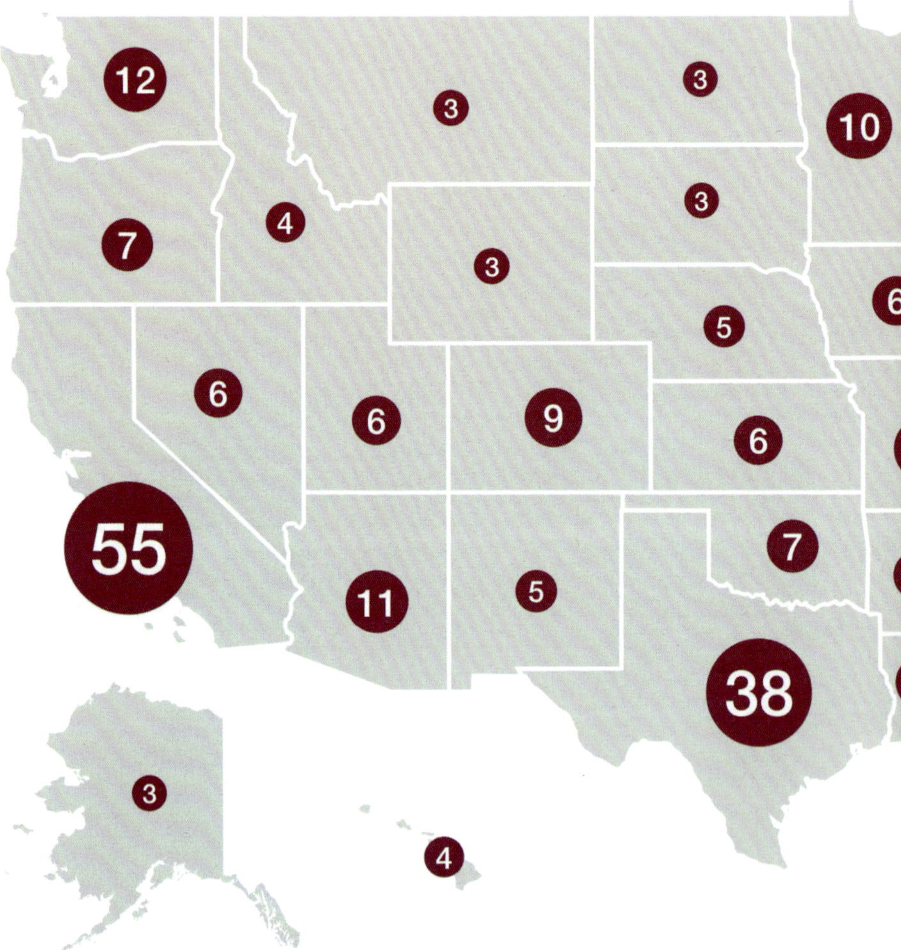

The Founders thought this was a way to make sure the votes of people who live in states with fewer people would still count. Because of the Electoral College, some presidents have been elected even though they did not win the popular vote. This is the vote of the majority of the people who voted. That is one reason some people think the Electoral College is not fair. They would like to see the candidate who gets the most votes win the presidential election.

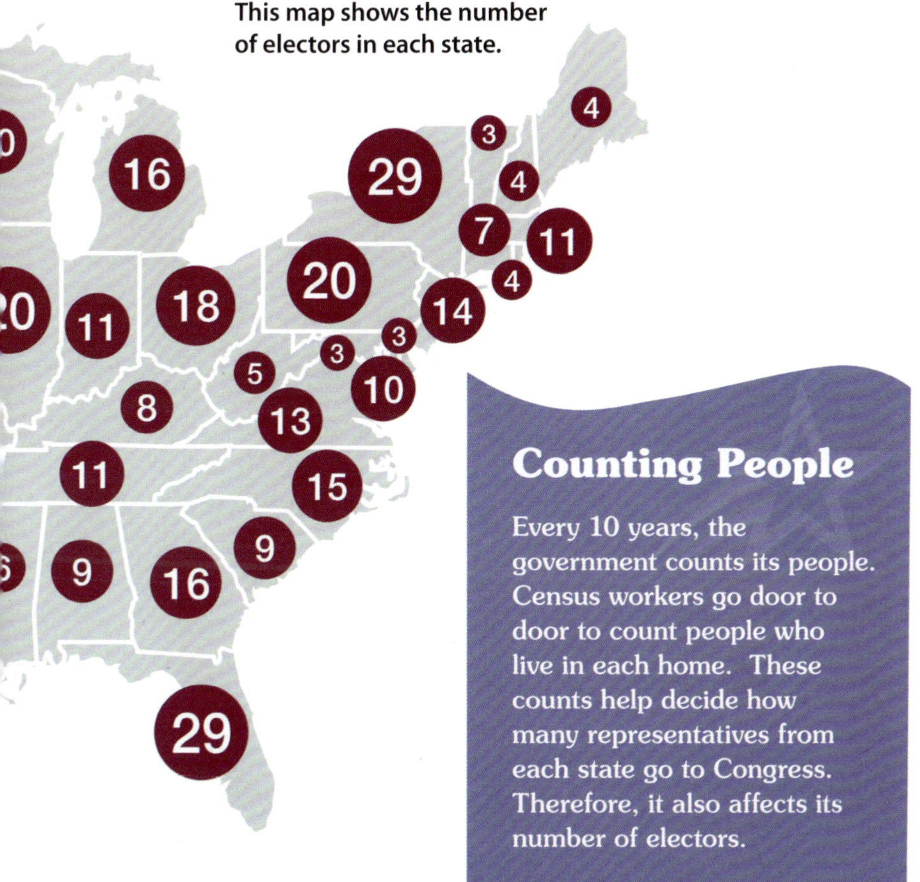

This map shows the number of electors in each state.

Counting People

Every 10 years, the government counts its people. Census workers go door to door to count people who live in each home. These counts help decide how many representatives from each state go to Congress. Therefore, it also affects its number of electors.

Where's the Money?

You have learned that state legislatures and the governor decide how to spend their state's budget. But where does that money come from? Taxes, of course!

Almost all states have a sales tax. It is typically four to eight cents on every dollar spent. For example, a T-shirt might cost $15. But if the state sales tax is 8 percent, the T-shirt will cost another $1.20. And that tax money belongs to the state. Some states have an income tax, too, which people have to pay every April. Anyone who owns a house pays property taxes to the state. Some taxes come right out of paychecks before they even get to workers. Legislators can also add taxes to the prices of necessities, such as gasoline.

State taxes support public resources such as libraries and parks.

Paying taxes can be hard. But remember that this money pays for important things. It pays for school systems and state colleges. It pays for police and fire departments. Tax money pays for parks and libraries. It pays for keeping air and water clean. And tax money pays the people who work for the state.

Local governments receive part of the state tax money, too. So, the way the state collects and budgets money affects people wherever they live.

When the Federal Government Pitches In

Sometimes, the federal government tells states to do specific things. For example, they may tell states to provide services for people with disabilities. These orders are called **mandates**. But if the federal government issues a mandate, it usually has to give the states the money to pay for implementing it.

Debate Over States' Rights Continues Today

At times, it seems as if the United States is made up of 50 smaller countries. In fact, some states are bigger than entire countries! For example, California's economy is worth more than $3 trillion. If California were a country, it would have the fifth largest economy in the world.

The balance of power between the federal government and the states has shifted over time. The 10th Amendment limits the powers of the federal government to those listed in the Constitution. The government passed this amendment in 1791 as part of the Bill of Rights. For instance, only the federal government can declare war. But most other powers belong to the states and their people.

This balance is to make sure the federal government does not turn into a dictatorship. The country fought hard for its freedom. Its founders wanted to preserve this freedom forever.

And, these rights have been tested during the country's history. The question of states' rights was key to the Civil War. Southern states wanted to keep slavery. The North wanted to end it. At issue was whether the federal government could end slavery in the states. The South lost the war. But the debate about states' rights continues today.

inside the Washington State Capitol

U.S. Bill of Rights

Take a State Capitol Tour

Most state capitol buildings are open for tours. Some tours allow people to sit in on and view actual debates among lawmakers. Even when capitol buildings close for tours, they often have virtual tours available online.

Map It!

You have read about how state governments are different from the federal government. But you have also seen how different state governments can be. One thing is the same in all states: their statehouses or capitol buildings are located in the state capital cities.

For this activity, follow these steps to study the state capitals:

1. Find a map that shows the location of the state capital for each of the 50 states.
2. Make a chart that shows the names of the states and capital cities.
3. Look up facts about each state, and figure out a symbol for each state. It could be the state flag, the state bird, the state flower, or even a state nickname.
4. Draw the symbol in your chart for each state.
5. What are your top five favorite states? Tell a friend why you chose each one as one of your favorites.

Mississippi State Capitol

Arizona State Capitol

New Hampshire State House

state name	capital	symbol
Illinois	Springfield	

Glossary

bankruptcy—financial failure caused by not having enough money to pay your debts

bicameral—having two parts

chambers—big rooms where members of a government group have meetings

civil—related to laws that describe a person's rights

compromise—a way of reaching agreement when both sides give up something they wanted

constitution—a document that describes the system of government for a country, a state, or an organization

electors—people authorized to vote in the Electoral College

legislators—people who make laws; members of a legislature

mandates—official orders

municipal—relating to the government of a city or a town

nuisance—something annoying

pandemic—a widespread outbreak of disease that quickly affects a lot of people across a wide area

political—relating to politics or government

preside—to be in charge of something

primary—a contest to select the candidates for a general election, especially for the role of president (in the United States)

recount—a new count

unicameral—having only one part; used to describe a government in which people who make laws are in one group

vacancy—open position

verdict—the decision made by a jury in a trial

veto—to not approve a new law or action

Index

inside the Virginia House of Representatives

Learn More!

Many governors go on to higher office. Franklin D. Roosevelt was one of the most well-known and influential leaders in U.S. history. Learn more about him by researching his life and career. Then, create an illustrated time line. Follow these steps:

- Start with his birth in 1882, and end with his death in 1945.
- Include his time in the New York State Senate.
- Note his elections to governor and president.
- Research his push for the New Deal, which helped the economy recover and helped people get back to work.
- Include World War II in your time line.